COUNTRY COMPARATOR
FOR ENCORPORATION AND
SUSTAINABLE INVESTING

Low-cost registration or low tax countries

LLC Comparator

Tim Claeyssens

Nform.work

LLC Comparator

About:

This paper compares the conditions for LLC incorporations in different promising countries.

The countries are chosen based on strategic location and on potential to bridge different markets in this more deglobalizing economic world.

LLC incorporation is always costly and has a yearly cost.

For this reason, starting with Sole Proprietorship first is always advisable.

The data (mainly numbers) in this paper are of an extremely dynamic nature and should be considered as proximate data rather.

Most data are from the last quarter of 2023.

The order of the countries is random.

For the UK and the USA, LLC registration per state comparison, a separate book would be needed.

10 Best & Worst States to Incorporate or Start a Business in 2022 (maxfilings.com)

Contents

LLC Comparator

LLC Comparator

LLC Comparator

Introduction

<u>A Limited Liability Company (LLC): What Is It?</u>

In the United States, a limited liability company (LLC) is a type of corporate structure that prevents its owners from becoming personally responsible for the debts or liabilities of the firm. Limited-liability corporations are hybrid entities that combine the features of a sole proprietorship or partnership with those of a corporation.

Whereas an LLC's limited liability is like that of a corporation, an LLC's members are not able to access flow-through taxation; that's a partnership feature.

KEY TAKEAWAYS

A corporate structure referred to as a limited liability company (LLC) protects its owners from being held personally liable for any obligations or debts of the business.

The laws governing LLCs differ from state to state.

An LLC can be formed by any company or person, with the significant exceptions of banks and insurance providers.

LLCs do not pay outright taxes on their profits.

Members receive a pass-through of their profits and losses, which they track on their own tax returns.

Overview of Limited Liability Companies (LLCs)

State statutes authorize limited liability firms, and each state has its own set of regulations regulating them. Members are the conventional term for LLC owners.

LLC Comparator

Since numerous states do not impose ownership restrictions, anybody can become a member, including corporations, individuals, foreign nationals, and even other LLCs. However, some organizations—such as banks and insurance companies—are prohibited from becoming LLCs.

A formal business structure known as an LLC necessitates filing articles of organization with the state. Compared to a corporation, an LLC is simpler to form and offers investors greater flexibility and security.

A formal business structure referred to as an LLC requires filing articles of organization with the state. Compared to a corporation, an LLC is simpler to form and offers investors greater flexibility and security.

LLCs have the option to forego direct federal tax payment. Rather, the owners' personal tax returns are where their earnings and losses are documented. The LLC may decide to be classified as something else entirely, like a corporation.

In the case that fraud occurs or a business neglect to comply with legal and reporting obligations, creditors could sue the members.

Establishing an LLC

While state-specific LLC rules differ, there are often commonalities. Choosing a name is the first task that owners or members must complete.

Following that, the articles of organization can be formalized and submitted to the state. Each LLC member's responsibilities, rights, and other obligations are outlined in these articles. The names and addresses of the LLC's members, the name of the registered agent, and the mission statement of the company are among the other details contained in the documents.

The organization's articles are submitted with a charge that is paid to the state directly. To receive an employer identification number (EIN), federal paperwork and associated payments must also be submitted.

The pros and cons of LLCs

The main motivation for LLC registration among business owners is to reduce their own and their partners' or investors' personal responsibility. Many see an LLC as a cross between a corporation, which has some liability protections, and a partnership, which is a simple commercial agreement between two or more owners.

LLCs have several benefits, but they also have a number of drawbacks. An LLC may need to be dissolved upon a member's death or bankruptcy, depending on state legislation. A corporation has an endless lifespan.

Partnership versus LLC

An LLC insulates the owners from the obligations and liabilities of the LLC by separating the commercial assets of the company from their personal assets. This is the main distinction between an LLC and a partnership.

It is legal for partnerships and LLCs to pass down their profits to their owners, along with the need to pay the associated taxes.

Only the amount invested can be deducted from their losses to offset other income. The LLC is required to file Form 1065 if it is set up as a partnership. (Form 1120 is filed if members have chosen to be handled as a company).

The remaining partners must dissolve the LLC and form a new one in the event of such an agreement.

What Is the Use of Limited Liability Companies (LLCs)?

The LLC offers these two key benefits:

It shields its owners from being held personally liable for the company's debts. The owner-investors' personal assets are not recoverable if the business files for bankruptcy or is sued.

It permits the direct transfer of all profits to the proprietors for personal income taxation.

By doing this, "double taxation" of the business and its owners is avoided.

What Are Some of the LLC Examples?

Few people are aware of how common LLCs are. Google's parent company, Alphabet, along with Johnson & Johnson, PepsiCo Inc., and Exxon Mobil Corp. are all LLCs.

Six

Numerous significantly smaller LLCs exist. Member-managed LLCs, family LLCs, and single proprietorship LLCs are some of the varieties.

Many medical groups are LLCs by registration. This lessens the likelihood that specific physicians will be held personally liable for awards for medical malpractice.

Do Corporations and Limited Liability Companies Pay Different Taxes?

Indeed. When a corporation makes profits, it is taxed twice: first at the corporate level and again when the gains are divided to the individual investors.

One of the most essential legal frameworks for launching a business is an LLC. The notion of limited liability states that the business's obligations and assets be kept apart from the owners' individual assets and debts. Creditors are only able to seize the business's assets if a firm files for bankruptcy; the owners' personal assets are shielded. LLCs also have several advantageous characteristics, including simple taxation and an incredibly straightforward registration process.

Many investors and companies complain about this "double taxation."

Conversely, limited liability firms permit the earnings to be distributed directly to the investors, resulting in a single taxation of the gains as part of the individuals' personal income.

The bottom lines

One of the most essential legal frameworks for launching a business is an LLC. The notion of limited liability states that the business's obligations and assets be kept apart from the owners' individual assets and debts. Creditors are only able to seize the business's assets if a firm files for bankruptcy; the owners' personal assets are shielded. LLCs also have several advantageous characteristics, including simple taxation and an incredibly straightforward registration process.

What is an LLC:

- Limited liability company.

This business form does protect the owners from loss of private capital mainly due to debt or lawsuits.

What does this paper assess:

This LLC comparison is all about assessing the advantages, prices and risks of opening or registering an LLC in a certain country.

Not all interesting facts are mentioned.

Are not mentioned: Double tax treaties, tax on foreign (investment) income and more.

Which countries and why?

We look for countries that give us access to as many markets as possible from a strategic location.

- Free trade agreements.
- Having bank accounts and reduced transfer fees doing business with these regions.

Country list: (unordered)

Switzerland, Hungary, Serbia, Montenegro, N-Macedonia, Slovenia, Georgia, Turkey, Cyprus, Armenia, Azerbaijan, Kazakhstan, Kyrgyzstan.

Pakistan, Hong Kong.

Country list:(ordered)

- Armenia
- Azerbaijan
- Bosnia and Herzegovina
- Bulgaria
- Egypt
- France
- Georgia
- IIong Kong
- Hungary
- Italy
- Kazakhstan
- Kyrgyzstan
- Montenegro
- Northern Cyprus (TRNC)
- N-Macedonia (North Macedonia)
- Pakistan
- Russia

I.L.C. Comparator

- Serbia
- Slovenia
- Switzerland
- Tunesia

Web search:

Easiest places to open a business?

Georgia and N-Macedonia

Affordable places to open a business?

Slovenia, Kazakhstan, and N-Macedonia

Best countries for LLC?

Hong Kong

Visa requirements for certain citizens (of these markets)

Kazakhstan Tourist visa for:

Serbia, Albania, Türkiye, Armenia, Georgia, Azerbaijan, Moldova, Belarus, Dubai, Oman, Pakistan (on demand)

Kyrgyzstan Tourist visa for:

Türkiye, Armenia, Georgia, Azerbaijan, Moldova, Belarus, Dubai, Oman.

LLC Comparator

Uzbekistan Tourist visa for:

Türkiye, Armenia, Georgia, Azerbaijan, Moldova, Belarus, Dubai, Oman.

China Tourist visa for:

Serbia, Albania, Bosnia, Türkiye, Armenia, Georgia, Azerbaijan, Belarus, Dubai, Oman.

Russian Tourist visa for:

Serbia, Montenegro, Bosnia H, Türkiye, Moldavia, Armenia, Georgia, Azerbaijan, Belarus, Dubai, Oman, Tunisia.

What do we compare?

Template:

Country:

Registration price:

Tax levels:

Free market agreements:

Country Commercial Guides (trade.gov)

Salary levels.

List of countries by average wage - Wikipedia

Reputation and Corruption levels.
LLC Comparator

<u>Citizenship options by company registration.</u>

<u>Foreign ownership possible?</u>

<u>Physical address needed?</u>

<u>Local hiring needed?</u>

<u>Web Reference for web sources.</u>

Country: Serbia

Registration price for LLC Company:

In Serbia, the minimum required founding capital for company registration is RSD 100, equivalent to less than €1.

Tax levels

Serbia offers a moderate taxation rate of 15%, and it has more than 64 avoidance of double taxation agreements in place.

The standard personal tax rate in this scenario is 10%. However, if an individual's earnings exceed three times the average salary, an additional tax rate of 10% is applied. For those earning six times the average salary, an extra 15% is imposed in addition to the previously mentioned tax rates.

Serbia has tax treaties with most countries within Europe, but the number of such treaties with countries outside (China, India, Brazil, South Africa, Australia, United States, Canada, Mexico, Japan, South Korea) of Europe is relatively limited.

Free market agreements:

Free Trade Agreements (ras.gov.rs)

European Union

Russian Federation

CEFTA

European Union, Iceland, Norway, Switzerland (including

Liechtenstein) or Turkey,

United States

Kazakhstan

Belarus

Visa requirements for certain citizens. (of these markets)

Simple tourist visa for citizens from:

China, Russia, Kazakhstan, Kyrgyzstan.

Salary levels.

1000$

Reputation and Corruption levels.

Complicated relationship with NATO since bombings in the

Balkan wars of the 90ties.

Citizenship options by company registration.

Residence permit by Company Formation » Welcome to Serbia

-> Yes, even possible EU citizenship later.

Foreign ownership?

Yes

LLC Comparator

<u>Physical address needed?</u>

<u>How to register a limited liability company in Serbia LLC (pavleski-law.rs)</u> seems yes through an Agency that can handle this.

<u>Local hiring needed?</u>

Yes

<u>Time needed for registration.</u>

5 working days.

<u>What documents do I need to provide?</u>

You only need to send us a copy of your passport.

<u>Company Formation in Serbia - Start Business</u>

<u>Start your LLC in Serbia » Welcome to Serbia</u>

1. Company & Bank accounts in just 15 days (about 2 weeks).

2. Low maintenance costs from 100 EUR/month

3. Ideal for international trading and international business optimization

4. Non-residents can be owners and directors

5. Low risk and the most accepted structure for the banks

6. Remote procedure

LLC Comparator

Completely <u>REMOTE</u> procedure?

Yes

Web Reference for web sourcing.

- **Serbian Business Registers Agency (SBRA):**
  - SBRA Official Website
- **Serbia Investment and Export Promotion Agency (SIEPA):**
  - SIEPA Official Website
- **Chamber of Commerce and Industry of Serbia:**
  - CCIS Official Website

Country: Georgia

LLC Registration price:

The cost of establishing an LLC in Georgia is $100, which covers the state filing fee for the required document, known as the Georgia Articles of Organization. These articles are submitted to the Secretary of State, also known as the Georgia Corporations Division. Upon approval, the Articles of Organization officially establish your LLC.

Tax levels:

Georgia imposes a state sales tax rate of 4.00 percent. Additionally, there is a maximum local sales tax rate of 5 percent. On average, when considering both state and local sales taxes, the combined rate in Georgia is 7.4 percent.

Taxes in Georgia are collected on both national and local levels. Personal Income tax in Georgia is collected at a flat rate of 20% on local-source income. Foreign-source personal income is tax-exempt.

Georgia has concluded agreements for avoidance of double taxation with 55 countries.

Free market agreements:

European Union

Commonwealth of Independent States (CIS)

(Russia, Ukraine, Belarus, Kazakhstan, Armenia, Azerbaijan)

European Free Trade Association (EFTA)

(Iceland, Liechtenstein, Norway, and Switzerland).

China

Türkiye

Salary levels.

$529

Reputation and Corruption levels.

In the 2022 Corruption Perceptions Index by Transparency International, where countries are scored on a scale from 0 ("highly corrupt") to 100 ("very clean"), Georgia received a score of 55.

Citizenship options by company registration.

No nationality is officially restricted.

https://passports.io/

Foreign ownership?

Yes

LLC Comparator

Physical address needed?

https://georgia.gov/register-llc >>>>>>>seems yes through an Agency that can handle this.

Local hiring needed?

Yes

Time needed for registration.

Approximately 1 to 2 business days.

What documents do I need to provide?

1. Name of the LLC or a valid name reservation number
2. Name and address of the person filing for the LLC
3. A valid email address
4. Mailing address of the principal office
5. Name and address of the registered agent
6. Name and address of each organizer
7. Any optional provisions you need to add to your articles of organization.
8. A form of payment. Depending on how you apply, your form of payment will be one of the following: credit card, check, cashier's check, or money order.

https://georgia.gov/register-llc

Complete Remote Process

LLC Comparator

Web Reference for web sourcing.

National Agency of Public Registry of Georgia:

NAPR Official Website

Georgian Chamber of Commerce and Industry:

Georgian CCI Official Website

Country: Kazakhstan

LLC Comparator

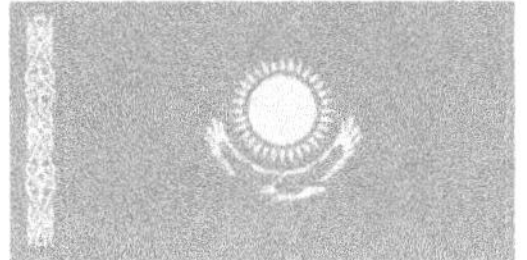

LLC Registration price:

In accordance with the tax legislation, the rate of the state fee for state registration (re-registration), state registration of termination of the activities of legal entities (including during reorganization in cases provided for by the legislation of the Republic of Kazakhstan), registration (re-registration), de-registration of their branches and representative offices, with the exception of commercial organizations is 6.5 fold f monthly assessment index.

The amount of the monthly assessment index from January 1, 2023 is KZT 3,450 (three thousand four hundred and fifty) tenge

Tax levels:

Residents are subject to a 10% personal income tax rate, while non-residents face a 15% rate. Legal entities are responsible for paying the social tax, equivalent to 11% of employees' salaries and in-kind benefits.

In January 2022, Kazakhstan entered various tax treaties with countries around the world to avoid double taxation. Countries included: (Russia, China, United States, Germany, United Kingdom, France, Türkiye, India, South Korea, Netherlands.

Free market agreements:

Eurasian Economic Union (EAEU)

LLC Comparator

Armenia, Belarus, Kyrgyzstan, and Russia

Commonwealth of Independent States (CIS) Free Trade Area

World Trade Organization (WTO)

Central Asia Free Trade Agreement (CAFTA)

Kazakhstan, Kyrgyzstan, Tajikistan, Turkmenistan, Uzbekistan

Salary levels.

$673

Reputation and Corruption levels.

Kazakhstan has made efforts to position itself as a key player in Central Asia, attracting foreign investment through economic reforms and infrastructure development.

In January 2022, the specific Corruption Perceptions Index (CPI) ranking for Kazakhstan 101 out 0f 180.

Citizenship options by company registration.

No https://egov.kz/cms/en

Foreign ownership?

Yes

Physical address needed?

Yes, a physical address is typically required for LLC registration in Kazakhstan.

LLC Comparator

Local hiring needed?

No

Time needed for registration.

5 to 10 working days.

What documents do I need to provide?

1. Application for Company Registration
2. Charter of the Company
3. Decision of the Founder (Founders) to Establish the Company
4. Founder's (Founders') Identity Documents
5. Document Confirming the Legal Address of the Company
6. Document Confirming the Payment of the State Duty for the Company Registration

Complete remote process

Yes

Web Reference for web sourcing.

Invest In Kazakhstan | Registration of Legal Entities

Қазақстан Республикасының Электрондық үкіметі | (egov.kz)

LLC Comparator

Country: Montenegro

LLC Registration price:

Registration fee of EUR 10 (USD 12.30) Administrative fee of EUR 12 (USD 14.80) for announcement in the Official Gazette. There is no minimum capital requirement.

Tax levels:

The tax rates are the same for citizens and foreigners: 9 to 15%.

Montenegro has signed so far **treaties double tax treaties** with: Albania, Belarus, Belgium, Bosnia and Herzegovina, Bulgaria, China, Croatia, Cyprus, Czech Republic, Denmark, Egypt, Finland, France, Germany, Hungary, Iran, Italy, Korea, Kuwait, Latonia, Macedonia, Malaysia, Moldavia, Holland, Norway, Poland, Romania, Russia, Slovakia, Slovenia, Sri Lanka, Sweden, Switzerland, Türkiye, Ukraine and United Kingdom.

Free market agreements:

Central European Free Trade Agreement (CEFTA)

Stabilization and Association Agreement (SAA) with the European Union

Free Trade Agreement with the European Free Trade Association (EFTA)

Agreement on the European Economic Area (EEA)

Salary levels.

$929

Reputation and Corruption levels.

Transparency International's Corruption Perceptions Index (CPI): In 2022, Montenegro scored 45 on a scale of 0 to 100, where 100 is "very clean" and 0 is "highly corrupt." This score ranked Montenegro 65th out of 180 countries, placing it in the lower middle tier globally.

Citizenship options by company registration.

10 years of continuous permanent residence, you can finally apply for Montenegrin citizenship.

https://www.lawyersmontenegro.eu/

Foreign ownership?

Yes

Physical address needed?

Yes, a physical address is required for an LLC company in Montenegro.

Local hiring needed?

Yes.

What documents do I need to provide?

1. Pay registration fees.
2. Check business name availability.
3. Prepare registration documents.
4. Register Limited Liability Company
5. Create company's seal.
6. Open company's bank account
7. Register with municipality.
8. Register with market inspection.
9. Obtain tax, health, and social security certificate.
10. Obtain VAT cash register.

https://montenegro.eregulations.org/procedure/23/23?l=en

Web Reference for web sourcing.

Montenegro's Agency for Business Registers website:

http://www.pretraga.crps.me:8083/

Montenegro's Ministry of Economy website:

LLC Comparator

https://www.gov.me/en/mek

The World Bank's Doing Business website:

https://data.worldbank.org/indicator/IC.BUS.EASE.XQ?locations=ME

LLC Comparator

Country: Bosnia and Herzegovina

LLC Registration price:

The fees for registering a company are as follows:

- d.o.o: BAM 200 (approximately)

- a.d.:   BAM 1,000 (approximately)

- Branch of a foreign company: BAM 400 (approximately)

Tax levels:

Income tax is applied at a flat tax rate of 10% on income from both employment, interest, royalties, and capital gains. Social Security applies to most employment income. The employee pays 33% of gross salary, while the employer contributes 10.5% in addition. The Value-added tax in Bosnia is 17% as standard rate.

Free market agreements:

Bosnia and Herzegovina (BiH) are a member of the Central European Free Trade Agreement (CEFTA). The agreement entered into force in November 2007 and includes Albania, Kosovo, North Macedonia, Moldova, Montenegro, Serbia, and

BiH. The agreement aims to support the economic development of the accession and pre-accession countries.

BiH also has a free trade agreement with Türkiye.

Salary levels.

1944 BAM/Month (1054.573 USD/Month)

Reputation and Corruption levels.

According to Transparency International's 2022 Corruption Perceptions Index, Bosnia and Herzegovina (BiH) scored 34 out of 100.

Citizenship options by company registration.

Obtaining Bosnian citizenship through company registration is not a direct or guaranteed path. Bosnian citizenship laws primarily focus on descent, long-term residency, and marriage to a Bosnian citizen. However, company registration and economic investment can indirectly support your citizenship application.

Foreign ownership?

Yes

Physical address needed?

Yes

<u>Local hiring needed?</u>

No

<u>Time needed for registration.</u>

4 to 6 weeks (about 1 and a half months),

<u>What documents do I need to provide?</u>

1. Establishment contract/decision (must be made by notary)

2. Payment of basic capital at a bank (bank by choice of founder)

3. Registration of the company at the competent court

4. Manufacturing the stamp

5. Opening a bank account

6. Registration of the company and employees at the tax administration

7. Obtaining the service permission

http://fipa.gov.ba/

<u>Web Reference for web sourcing.</u>

fipa.gov.ba

https://komorabih.ba/en/

http://www.bembassy.org/visa.html

LLC Comparator

Country: Switzerland

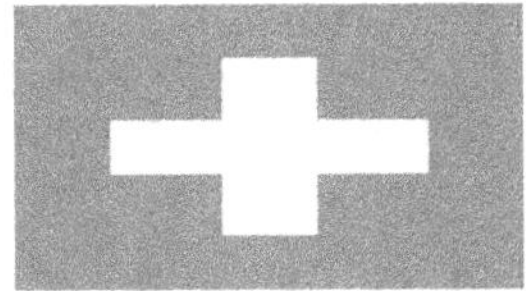

LLC Registration price:

The required base registration fee is CHF 230-240. Demanded Notary fees are to be between CHF 999 and CHF 3,000.

Tax levels:

The maximum overall rate of federal income tax is 11.5%. The various cantonal and municipal taxes are also levied at progressive rates, with a maximum combined cantonal and municipal rate of approximately 36%. In addition, cantonal and municipal net wealth taxes are levied.

Free market agreements:

Switzerland has a network of 33 free trade agreements (FTAs) with 43 partners worldwide. These FTAs aim to reduce tariffs and other trade barriers, making it easier for Swiss businesses to export their goods and services to partner countries. They also promote investment and economic cooperation between Switzerland and its trading partners.

European Union (EU) - China

North American Free Trade Agreement (NAFTA)

ASEAN - China Free Trade Area

United States - Mexico-Canada Agreement (USMCA)

EU - Japan Economic Partnership Agreement

EU - Vietnam Free Trade Agreement (EVFTA)

https://www.seco.admin.ch/seco/en/home.html

https://www.wto.org/english/thewto_e/countries_e/switzerland_e.htm

Salary levels.

$ 8,111

Reputation and Corruption levels.

Switzerland ranked seventh for a second year in a row in Transparency International's Corruption Perception Index, but its overall score marks a historic low for the country.

Citizenship options by company registration.

No, simply registering a company in Switzerland does not automatically grant you citizenship.

https://www.sem.admin.ch/sem/en/home.html

Foreign ownership?

No

LLC Comparator

<u>Physical address needed?</u>

Yes

<u>Local hiring needed?</u>

No

<u>Time needed for registration.</u>

2 to 3 weeks

<u>What documents do I need to provide?</u>

1. Articles of Association (Statutes):
   - Name and registered office of the company
   - Purpose of the company
   - Share capital and share structure.
   - Management structure (board of directors, managing directors)
   - Duties and powers of the shareholders and directors
   - Profit distribution and liquidation procedures
2. Memorandum of Association (Gründungsurkunde):
   - Names and addresses of the founders.
   - Confirmation of the founders' intention to establish the company.
   - Details of the share capital contributions.

3. Specimen Signatures:

- Signed specimen signature cards of all directors and authorized signatories.

4. Share Capital Deposit:

- Evidence of payment of the minimum share capital (20,000 CHF for an LLC) into a Swiss bank account

5. Identification Documents:

- Passport or identity card copies of all directors and shareholders

- In some cases, proof of residence for directors and shareholders

6. Registration Application:

- Completed registration application form, signed by all directors.

7. Power of Attorney (if applicable):

- Power of attorney if a third party is handling the registration process.

For this purpose, the Government specially designed a platform on which you complete all the process remotely.

https://www.easygov.swiss/easygov/#/

Web Reference for web sourcing.

https://handelsregister.ch/

https://www.s-ge.com/en/sbh

LLC Comparator

https://www.englishforum.ch/

https://newco.ch/en

https://www.easygov.swiss/easygov/#/

LLC Comparator

Country: Hungary

LLC Registration price:

The registration fee for capital-share limited liability companies is about 100,000 HUF.

Tax levels:

Tax assessment in Hungary is required by both the public and nearby legislatures. Charge income in Hungary remained at 38.4% of Gross domestic product in 2017. The main income sources incorporate the annual expense, Government backed retirement, corporate duty and the worth added charge, which are totally applied at the public level. Among the complete expense pay the proportion of neighborhood charges is exclusively 5% while the EU normal is 30%.

Income tax in Hungary is levied at a flat rate of 15%

Free market agreements:

Hungary has a preferential trade agreement with the EU and free trade agreements with the European Free Trade Area (EFTA), Central European neighbors (CEFTA), Turkey, and

Israel. Hungary has also signed more than 80 bilateral agreements with other countries.

Bilateral agreements:

- Japan: Comprehensive Free Trade Agreement (2013)
- Canada: Comprehensive Economic and Trade Agreement (CETA) (2017)

Salary levels.

$ 1,189

Reputation and Corruption levels.

According to a survey of businessmen in 85 countries, Hungary is the 33rd least corrupt country.

Citizenship options by company registration.

No, direct citizenship is given by Hungary.

Immigration services>>>>.http://www.bmbah.hu/

Foreign ownership?

Yes

Physical address needed?

Yes

Hungarian law requires a registered agent (kft. székhelyszolgáltató) if you're not physically present in Hungary.

Local hiring needed?

No

Time needed for registration.

3 weeks

What documents do I need to provide?

The application for the company registers at the Court must contain.

1. A commercial license.

2. Documents of incorporation.

3. A registered address

4. A unique name for company

5. The activity and the type of company

6. Opening bank account

7. An accountant

The file must also include the receipt from the bank account.

https://www.companyregister.hu/

LLC Comparator

Web Reference for web sourcing.

https://tarhely.gov.hu/ckp-regisztracio/tajekoztato.html

https://2015-2019.kormany.hu/en/ministry-of-justice/contacts

https://nav.gov.hu/

Some Organizations and resources.

Hungarian Investment Promotion Agency (HIPA)

https://hipa.hu/

Hungarian Chamber of Commerce and Industry (MKIK)

https://mkik.hu/

Country: North Cyprus

LLC Registration price:

The government registration fee is €205

Tax levels:

Taxes in Cyprus are collected by both the focal and nearby states. Tax income remained at 39.2% of gross domestic product in 2012. The main income sources are the annual expense, federal retirement aide, value-added charge, and corporate assessment, which are completely gathered by the focal government.

Personal duty is exacted at an ever-evolving rate. Current sections differ from 0% to 35% in the duty rates for 2014.

Free market agreements

The Turkish Republic of Northern Cyprus (TRNC), as a state with limited international recognition, does not officially have any free trade agreements (FTAs) with other countries. This is primarily due to its lack of widespread recognition and the ongoing political situation regarding its sovereignty.

https://www.canlii.org/

Salary levels.

$ 2,316

Reputation and Corruption levels.

In 2022, the TRNC scored 27 out of 100 on Transparency International's CPI, ranking 140th out of 180 countries.

Citizenship options by company registration.

No, Direct citizenship is provided by North Cyprus >>>>>>>https://www.erginellaw.com/

Foreign ownership?

Yes

Physical address needed?

Yes

Local hiring needed?

No

Time needed for registration.

5 business days

What documents do I need to provide?

1. SELECT A COMPANY NAME

LLC Comparator

2. WRITE THE MEMORANDUM AND ARTICLES OF ASSOCIATION

3. COMPLETE COMPANY INCORPORATION FORMS

4. PROVIDE CERTAIN INFORMATION FOR EACH FOREIGN SHAREHOLDER

   a. Certified copy of the passport

   b. Original Police Clearance Certificate issued by the country of citizenship.

   c. Residence Certificate issued by a local Muhtar stating residential address in the TRNC

5. PROVIDE TAX SECURITY CERTIFICATE FOR EACH DIRECTOR

6. DEPOSIT THE CAPITAL SHARE TO A BANK IN NORTHERN CYPRUS

Web Reference for web sourcing.

Erginel Law:

https://www.erginellaw.com/

Fidesta Ltd:

https://rightax.com.cy/cyprus-company-formation-steps/

North Cyprus Company Formation:

https://www.northcypruscompany.com/north-cyprus-company-incorporation/

LLC Comparator

Country: Bulgaria

LLC Registration price:

According to workinbulgaria.net, the registration fee for a Limited Liability Company (OOD) in Bulgaria is EUR 55. The reservation of a company name costs EUR 20

Tax levels:

Tax rate for Bulgarians is 10% regardless of their income and whether they live and work in Bulgaria or abroad. Self-employment income is also charged with 10% tax. Non-resident individuals are taxed only on their income from sources in Bulgaria.

Free market agreements:

Bulgaria became a member of the World Trade Organization in 1996,

Joined the Central European Free Trade Agreement (CEFTA) in 1999

Joined the EU in 2007.

Bulgaria has free trade agreements with:

China (1995),

Turkey (1999),

Macedonia (1999),

Israel (2002),

Albania (2003),

Serbia and Montenegro (2004),

Bosnia and Herzegovina (2004), and

Moldova (2004).

Salary levels.

$ 947

Reputation and Corruption levels.

Bulgaria ranked 72nd among the 180 countries in the Index, where the country ranked first is perceived to have the most honest public sector.

Citizenship options by company registration.

No, direct citizenship is offered

>>>>>>>https://www.bulgarianlegal.com/

Foreign ownership?

No

Physical address needed?

Yes

LLC Comparator

<u>Local hiring needed?</u>

No

<u>Time needed for registration.</u>

3–5 days

<u>What documents do I need to provide?</u>

1. Application for Registration:

- Obtain this from the Registry Agency.
- Ensure it completed accurately and in Bulgarian.

2. Name Certificate:

- This document confirms the company's chosen name is available.
- Acquire it from the Registry Agency.

3. Constituent Act:

This outlines the company's structure and operations.

It includes:
- Name and address
- Business activities

- o   Share capital.
- o   Management structure
- o   Profit distribution
- o   Dispute resolution procedures
- It must be notarized.

4. Signature Specimen:

- This is a sample of the director's signature.
- It must be notarized.
-

5. Identification Documents:

- Copies of passports or ID cards for all founders and directors.

6. Bank Statement:

- This confirms the deposit of the minimum share capital (2 BGN).

7. Declaration of Consent from Director:

- This document states the director accepts the position and their signature will represent the company.
- It must be notarized.

8. Declarations of Circumstances:

- These confirm the accuracy of the information provided to the Trade Register.
- Signed by founders and directors, but not requiring notarization.

LLC Comparator

Additional Documents (if applicable):

- Power of Attorney: If a third party is handling registration.

- Legalized Corporate Documents: If founders are legal entities.

- Licenses or Permits: Required for specific business activities.

- Documents must be in Bulgarian or officially translated.

- Notarization is required for specific documents.

- Professional assistance is recommended to ensure compliance.

Web Reference for web sourcing

Ministry of Foreign Affairs of Bulgaria:

https://www.mfa.bg/en/services-travel/consular-services/travel-bulgaria/visa-bulgaria

Unified Trade Register of the Bulgarian Chamber of Commerce and Industry (BCCI):

https://www.bcci.bg/trade-it-it.html

Ministry of Justice:

https://justice.government.bg/

e-Bulgaria Portal:

https://www.egov.bg/

LLC Comparator

Country: North-Macedonia

LLC Registration price:

The average fee for registering a North Macedonia LLC is €16,000.

Tax levels:

Income tax is paid at a progressive rate of 10% for the earned income up to 1.080. 000 MKD per year, and of 18% for the earned income above this threshold, for any labor income earned. Income tax is paid at a flat rate of 15% for any capital income earned. A tax haven in Europe, North Macedonia has implemented a flat tax rate that has seen progressive cuts.

In the long-term, the North Macedonia Personal Income Tax Rate is projected to trend **around 10.00 percent in 2025.**

Free market agreements:

North Macedonia, nestled in the heart of the Balkans, is actively expanding its reach through a network of free trade agreements (FTAs). These agreements eliminate or reduce tariffs and other trade barriers, fostering greater economic integration and boosting trade opportunities for businesses in North Macedonia and its partner countries.

Here's a closer look at some of the key FTAs that North Macedonia has signed:

1. Central European Free Trade Agreement (CEFTA):

- Established in 2006, CEFTA is a regional FTA encompassing Albania, Bosnia and Herzegovina, Kosovo, Moldova, Montenegro, North Macedonia, Serbia, and (until 2013) Croatia.

- It eliminates tariffs on most industrial goods and gradually reduces tariffs on agricultural products.
- Provides duty-free access to a market of over 45 million consumers.

2. Stabilization and Association Agreement (SAA) with the European Union (EU):

- Signed in 2001, the SAA is a comprehensive agreement that covers trade, political cooperation, and other areas.
- The trade component of the SAA establishes a preferential trade arrangement, granting duty-free

access for most North Macedonian industrial goods to the EU market of over 500 million consumers.

- The SAA also provides for a gradual reduction of tariffs on EU goods entering North Macedonia.

3. European Free Trade Association (EFTA) Agreement:

- Signed in 2000, the EFTA Agreement covers trade in industrial goods and fish and marine products with Iceland, Norway, Switzerland, and Liechtenstein.
- Eliminates tariffs on most industrial goods and provides substantial concessions on fish and marine products.
- Offers access to a market of over 13 million consumers.

4. Bilateral Free Trade Agreement with Turkey:

- Signed in 1999, the FTA with Turkey eliminates tariffs on most industrial goods and gradually reduces tariffs on agricultural products.
- Provides access to a market of over 83 million consumers.

https://www.trade.gov/country-commercial-guides/north-macedonia-trade-agreements

LLC Comparator

5. Bilateral Free Trade Agreement with Ukraine:

- Signed in 2016, the FTA with Ukraine eliminates tariffs on most industrial goods and gradually reduces tariffs on agricultural products.

- Provides access to a market of over 44 million consumers.

Salary levels.

$813

Reputation and Corruption levels.

According to Transparency International's 2022 Corruption Perceptions Index, North Macedonia scored 40 out of 100, ranking 85th out of 180 countries.

Citizenship options by company registration.

Yes, citizenship is offer after company registration >>>>>>>https://investnorthmacedonia.gov.mk

Foreign ownership?

Yes

Physical address needed?

Yes

Local hiring needed?

No

Time needed for registration.

One-Stop-Shop system through which company formation in Macedonia can normally be completed within four hours (2-3 business days in practice).

What documents do I need to provide?

Documents must comprise information about:

- Name of the company
- Main activity/core business (for example: Trade with....)
- Headquarter of the company in Macedonia
- Name of the bank in which the company will have a bank account.
- The names of the owners. For physical person: name, surname, address of living, Copy of passport and ID card. For the legal entity: Current Status of the company issued by Trade register at their native country (Act of establishing on the company of the owner) not older than 3 months.
- Authorized representative – manager: Copy of the passport and ID card

- Initial capital (minimum 5.000 euro)
- The information about the owner's liabilities and how the profits are distributed, in accordance with the shares.

<u>Web Reference for web sourcing.</u>

Invest North Macedonia:

https://investnorthmacedonia.gov.mk/registering-a-company/

Central Register of North Macedonia:

https://portal.registryagency.bg/en/

LLC Comparator

Country: Russia

LLC Registration price:

The average cost of setting up a limited liability company (LLC) in Russia is around 200,000 to 400,000 rubles (approximately $2,700 to $5,400 USD).

Tax Levels:

Russia's tax system is considered relatively simple compared to other developed countries, with a focus on a flat personal income tax rate and a value-added tax (VAT). Here's a breakdown of the main tax levels in Russia:

Personal Income Tax:

- Flat rate of 13% on most income, including salaries, wages, pensions, and interest income.
- Tax deductions: Available for certain expenses like medical treatment, education, and charitable donations.
- Non-residents: Subject to a 30% income tax rate, except for dividends (15%).

Value Added Tax (VAT):

- Standard rate of 20% on most goods and services.

- Reduced rates of 10% and 0% apply to certain essential goods and services, such as food and medicine.

Other Taxes:

- Corporate income tax: 20% for most businesses, with lower rates for small businesses and certain industries.
- Social security contributions: 3% for employees and 22% for employers.

Free market agreements:

- Eurasian Economic Union (EAEU): Russia is a founding member of the EAEU and is party to trade agreements with Vietnam, Iran, Singapore, and Serbia. The EAEU also has a trade cooperation agreement with China and is negotiating with India, Israel, and Egypt.
- Commonwealth of Independent States Free Trade Area (CISFTA): This free-trade area includes Russia, Ukraine, Belarus, Uzbekistan, Moldova, Armenia, Kyrgyzstan, Kazakhstan, and Tajikistan.
- Ukraine: Russia has had a free trade agreement with Ukraine since 1994.

Russia has also been a member of the WTO since 2012

Salary levels.

$ 2,159

Reputation and Corruption levels.

According to a 2021 report, Russia scored 29 out of 100 points on a scale that measures perceived corruption. This score indicates a high level of perceived corruption, ranking Russia 136 out of 180 countries.

Citizenship options by company registration.

No direct citizenship is offer by Russia >>>>>http://russia-ic.com/services/legalservices

Foreign ownership?

Yes

Physical address needed?

Yes

Local hiring needed?

No

Time needed for registration.

2–4 weeks

What documents do I need to provide?

1. Application for Registration:

- This form is available from the Federal Tax Service of Russia (FTS) and can be submitted online or in person.

- It includes basic information about the LLC, such as its name, address, activities, and founders.

2. Charter of the LLC:

- This document outlines the company's structure, governance, and operations.

- It should specify the LLC's name, address, activities, share capital, management structure, and dispute resolution procedures.

3. Decision of the Founders to Establish the LLC:

- This document records the founders' agreement to create the LLC and their approval of the company's charter.

- It should list the names and signatures of all founders.

4. Minutes of the Founders' Meeting (if applicable):

- If a meeting of the founders was held to discuss the LLC's formation, minutes of that meeting should be provided.

5. Passports or Identity Documents of Founders:

- Copies of the founders' passports or other identification documents are required to verify their identities.
- If a founder is a foreign entity, a certified copy of its registration documents will be needed.

6. Bank Statement Confirming Share Capital Payment:

- This statement shows that the LLC's share capital has been deposited into a bank account.
- The minimum share capital for an LLC in Russia is 10,000 rubles (approximately $165 as of June 2023).

7. Power of Attorney (if applicable):

- If a representative is handling the registration on behalf of the founders, a power of attorney authorizing them to act on the founders' behalf is necessary.

8. Registration Fee Payment Receipt:

- A receipt showing payment of the state registration fee, which is currently 4,000 rubles (approximately $66 as of June 2023).

Web Reference for web sourcing.

Federal Tax Service of Russia (FTS):

https://nalog.gov.ru/: https://nalog.gov.ru/

Federal Portal for State Services:

https://www.gosuslugi.ru/:
https://www.gosuslugi.ru/

Country: Kyrgyzstan

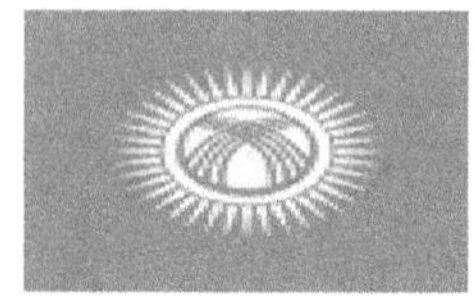

LLC Registration price:

The fee for registering a company is: LLC: KGS 1,000 (approximately $12)

Tax levels:

Kyrgyzstan's tax-to-GDP ratio was 20.0% in 2021, above the Asia and Pacific (29) average of 19.8% by 0.3 percentage points. It was below the OECD average (34.1%) by 14.1 percentage points. The tax-to-GDP ratio in Kyrgyzstan increased by 2.6 percentage points from 17.4% in 2020 to 20.0% in 2021.

Free market agreements:

Bilateral Investment Treaties:

- Extensive network with over 20 countries including US, China, UK, India, Pakistan.
- US-Kyrgyz Republic treaty has been in force since 1994.

US Trade Support:

- The Generalized System of Preferences (GSP) program allows duty-free exports of 3,500 products to the US.
- Trade and Investment Framework Agreement (TIFA) for addressing trade issues and regional collaboration.
- The Commercial Law Development Program (CLDP) promotes trade liberalization and improves the business environment.

Eurasian Economic Union (EAEU) Membership:

- Provides access to a large market of 180 million people.
- Free movement of labor, capital, and goods within the EAEU.

Double Taxation Treaties:

- Treaty with US remains in effect.
- Extensive network of treaties with other countries to avoid double taxation.

https://www.trade.gov/country-commercial-guides/kyrgyz-republic-trade-agreements

Salary levels.

$ 228

LLC Comparator

Reputation and Corruption levels.

Kyrgyzstan is ranked 140th out of 180 countries in Transparency International's 2022 Corruption Perceptions Index.

Citizenship options by company registration.

No direct citizenship is given >>>>>. https://www.migrant.kg/

Foreign ownership?

Yes

Physical address needed?

Yes

Local hiring needed?

No

Time needed for registration.

10 business days

What documents do I need to provide?

Company name.

Registered address (can be provided by us).

Participant's data (name, citizenship, passport/company's constituent documents).

Amount of the authorized capital.

LLC Comparator

Kinds of activities.

Chosen bank in Kyrgyzstan and kinds of accounts to be opened therewith.

Selection of the taxation system (common, simplified).

Other documents and data at the request of the experts of ALPS & CHASE. *

Web Reference for web sourcing.

Ministry of Justice of the Kyrgyz Republic:

http://minjust.gov.kg/ru/ (Kyrgyz, but you can use Google Translate

Registration of Legal Entities in the Kyrgyz Republic:

http://www.k-a.kg/eng/faq/registration-legal-entities-kyrgyz-republic-8-frequently-asked-questions

Country: Armenia

LLC Registration price:

The standard registration fee for an LLC in Armenia is 8,000 drams, which is about $17.

Tax levels:

The Personal Income Tax Rate in Armenia stands at 20 percent. Personal Income Tax Rate in Armenia averaged 25.33 percent from 2003 until 2023, reaching an all-time high of 36.00 percent in 2014 and a record low of 20.00 percent in 2004.

Free market agreements:

Armenia has several free trade agreements in place, both bilateral and multilateral. Here are some key points to know:

Armenia's Membership in Trade Blocs:

- Eurasian Economic Union (EAEU): Armenia joined the EAEU in 2015, gaining free trade access to Russia, Belarus, Kazakhstan, Kyrgyzstan, and Tajikistan.

- World Trade Organization (WTO): Armenia has been a member of the WTO since 2003, enjoying benefits like non-discrimination in trade policies and access to dispute settlement mechanisms.

Bilateral Free Trade Agreements:

- Georgia: Armenia has a free trade agreement with its neighboring Georgia, facilitating trade in goods and services.
- Switzerland: A free trade agreement with Switzerland is currently under negotiation and expected to boost trade between the two countries.

Other Trade Agreements:

- Comprehensive and Enhanced Partnership Agreement (CEPA) with the European Union: While not a free trade agreement in the strictest sense, the CEPA significantly liberalizes trade between Armenia and the EU by reducing tariffs and other barriers.
- Generalized System of Preferences (GSP): Armenia also benefits from preferential access to markets like the US and EU under their respective GSP programs.

Salary levels.

$541

Reputation and Corruption levels.

According to the 2022 Corruption Perception Index (CPI), Armenia ranks 63rd out of 180 countries, scoring 46 out of 100.

Citizenship options by company registration.

No direct citizenship is granted>>>>

https://www.facebook.com/armenia.ms >

Foreign ownership?

Yes

Physical address needed?

Yes

Local hiring needed?

Yes

Time needed for registration.

10 weeks for total process

What documents do I need to provide?

The founders' decision to create the LLC.

LLC Comparator

The LLC's charter.

A notarized copy of the passport of the LLC participant

A notarized copy of the passport of the LLC head

A notarized translation of the passport into Armenian if the applicant is a foreigner.

An application

The company's registration address

Personal information about the executive, including their passport.

A Beneficial Ownership Certificate

Web Reference for web sourcing.

Ministry of Justice of the Republic of Armenia: https://www.moj.am/en

State Register of Legal Entities and Movable Property: https://www.e-register.am/en/

Tashir Law Firm: https://tlclawfirm.com/

Country: Italy

LLC Registration price:

The company incorporation fee in Italy is approximately 2300 Euros.

Tax levels:

The income tax is progressive and varies from 23 to 43%. Inheritance and gift taxes in Italy are among the lowest in Europe — the rate is between 4 and 8%. The main taxes for companies in Italy are corporate income tax of 24%, regional production tax of around 3.9%, and 22% VAT.

Free market agreements:

Italy, as a member of the European Union, participates in all the EU's free trade agreements. These agreements cover a wide range of countries and territories and offer preferential terms for trade in goods and services.

Here are some of the most notable free trade agreements that Italy benefits from:

- North American Free Trade Agreement (NAFTA):

- Comprehensive Economic and Trade Agreement (CETA):
- Japan-EU Economic Partnership Agreement (JAEPA):
- Korea-EU Free Trade Agreement (KORUS):
- EU-Chile Association Agreement:

Salary levels.

$ 2,763

Reputation and Corruption levels.

According to Transparency International's 2022 Corruption Perceptions Index, Italy scored 56 out of 100, ranking 41st out of 180 countries.

Citizenship options by company registration.

No direct citizenship is given>>>>>
https://www.cittadinanza.biz/servizio-civile-ministero-dellinterno-e-cittadinanza-italiana/.

Foreign ownership?

Yes

Physical address needed?

Yes

Local hiring needed?

No
LLC Comparator

Time needed for registration.

5-6 working days.

What documents do I need to provide?

- Personal information, such as your ID or passport

- If you're a foreign company, your Certificate of Registration and incorporation documents.

- The company's establishment documents, which are drafted by an Italian public notary.

- Register with the Italian Tax Authorities to get a tax identification number.

- Shareholders sign the Articles of Association in front of a public notary.

- Arrange articles of association and memorandum of association

- Obtain an Italian tax code.

- Open a local bank account.

- Register for VAT

- File with the Registrar of Companies

- The minimum share capital required to open an SRL is 10,000 euros.

- The limited liability company must have a registered office in Italy.

<u>Web Reference for web sourcing.</u>

Registro Imprese (Business Register)

<u>https://www.registroimprese.it/</u>:

Registro Imprese (Business Register)

LLC Comparator

Country: France

LLC Registration price:

The cost of registering with your company online starts from 550 Euros.

Tax levels:

The income tax rate in France is progressive, meaning it increases with your income. The rates range from 0% to 45%, with an additional surtax of 3% or 4% on high incomes.

All employees and self-employed individuals in France must pay social security contributions, which fund the country's healthcare, unemployment, and retirement systems. The contribution rate is based on your income and can range from 15% to 24% for employees and 35% to 47% for employers.

France has a standard VAT rate of 20%, but there are also reduced rates for certain goods and services, such as food and essential items.

Free market agreements:

France, as a key player in the European Union, enjoys a vast network of free trade agreements (FTAs) that connect it to economies around the globe.

- EU-wide FTAs: First and foremost, France benefits from the extensive network of FTAs negotiated by the European Union. These agreements cover a wide range of countries and territories, from Canada and Mexico to Japan and Vietnam, granting preferential access to markets for French exports.
- Bilateral FTAs: France also pursues its own independent FTAs, further expanding its trade reach. Notable examples include agreements with South Korea, Singapore, and Mercosur (a South American trade bloc), which open doors to diverse and dynamic economies.

Salary levels.

$ 3,655

Reputation and Corruption levels.

France ranked 21st among the 180 countries in the Index, where the country ranked first is perceived to have the most honest public sector.

Citizenship options by company registration.

Foreign ownership?

Yes

Physical address needed?

Yes

Local hiring needed?

No

Time needed for registration.

2 to 4 weeks

What documents do I need to provide?

- Business Registration Certificate. ...
- Tax Identification Number. ...
- Proof of Legal Address for the Business. ...
- ID or Passport for Each Business Owner. ...
- Articles of Association or Other Incorporation Documents. ...
- Initial Capital Contribution Certificate.

Web Reference for web sourcing.

Guichet unique des formalités des entreprises (Guichet unique)

https://www.guichet-entreprises.fr/en/.

LLC Comparator

French Chamber of Commerce and Industry (CCI):

https://www.businessfrance.fr/about-us-our-partners-cci-de-france

Business France:

https://www.businessfrance.fr/en/home

LLC Comparator

Country: Tunisia

LLC Registration price:

The incorporation costs for a company in its first year are US\$6,700.

Tax levels:

Direct Taxes:

- Individual Income Tax: Progressive rates ranging from 0% to 35.5%, with thresholds that vary depending on family size and income sources.

- Corporate Income Tax: Generally, at a flat rate of 15%, with exceptions for specific industries and activities.

- Social Solidarity Contribution: An additional 1% levy on taxable income for most taxpayers, with higher rates for certain sectors like banks and insurance companies.

Indirect Taxes:

- Value Added Tax (VAT): Standard rate of 19%, with reduced rates (7% and 13%) for specific goods and services like necessities, pharmaceutical products, and tourism activities.

- Hotel Residency Tax: Applies to guests older than 12 years old, at various rates depending on hotel classification and location.
- Excise Taxes: Levied on a limited range of goods, such as tobacco, alcohol, and fuel.

Tax Incentives:

The Tunisian government offers various tax incentives to promote investment and economic development, including:

- Tax holidays: Exemptions from corporate income tax for a specific period for new businesses in certain sectors.
- Accelerated depreciation: Allows businesses to deduct the cost of certain assets from their taxable income at a faster rate.
- Export tax rebate: Refunds companies a portion of the VAT they paid on exported goods.

Free market agreements:

Tunisia, strategically located in North Africa, plays a key role in regional and international trade. To facilitate these exchanges.

LLC Comparator

- European Union (EU): Tunisia's most important FTA is its Association Agreement with the EU, operational since 1998. This agreement established a free trade area for industrial goods, with tariffs gradually eliminated over a 12-year period. Notably, it remains crucial for approximately 70% of Tunisia's trade.

- Agadir Agreement: This framework agreement, signed in 2004, promotes free trade among Tunisia, Egypt, Jordan, and Morocco. It has facilitated increased inter-regional trade within North Africa.

Bilateral Agreements:

- Turkey: The 2004 Association Agreement between Tunisia and Turkey offers substantial tariff reductions and eliminates barriers for specific agricultural products. This agreement has boosted bilateral trade significantly.

- Algeria and Libya: Separate bilateral FTAs exist with these neighboring countries. However, trade with Algeria remains low, and trade with Libya has dropped significantly since the Arab Spring, highlighting the complexities of regional dynamics.

Salary levels.

$120

Reputation and Corruption levels.

In 2022, Tunisia scored 40 out of 100 on the CPI, ranking 85th out of 180 countries.

Citizenship options by company registration.

No direct citizenship is given
>>>>>>>>>https://www.diplomatie.gov.tn/

Foreign ownership?

Yes

Physical address needed?

Yes

Local hiring needed?

No

Time needed for registration.

5 weeks.

What documents do I need to provide?

- Identification documents: Passports, national ID cards, and proof of address for shareholders, directors, and beneficial owners

- Company documents: Memorandum and Articles of Association, project declaration certificate, and statutes
- Business documents: Declaration of commencement of business with the tax administration, tax identification card, and document providing the headquarters address.
- Company address: Copy of the rent agreement, and proof of a local registered office address
- Bank documents: Receipts of bank account opening and bank receipts of the capital account of the company.
- Other documents: APII declaration copies, fiscal stamp, and administrative authorization

Web Reference for web sourcing.

Guichet Unique des Formalités des Entreprises (GUFE):

http://fr.tunisie.gov.tn/

Tunisian Ministry of Justice:

https://www.justice.gov.tn/index.php?id=11&L=3

Agence de Promotion des Investissements Etrangers (API):

http://www.investintunisia.tn/Fr/notre-mission_11_203

Country: Azerbaijan

LLC Registration price:

Registering a company in Azerbaijan can cost between 60 and 400 AZN (approximately USD 35 to USD 235).

Tax levels:

Azerbaijan's tax system is relatively simple and straightforward compared to other countries in the region. The main types of taxes levied in Azerbaijan include:

Individual Income Tax:

- Progressive tax rates ranging from 14% to 25%, depending on the level of income.
- The first AZN 2,500 of monthly income is tax-free.
- Above AZN 2,500, a fixed amount of AZN 350 is added to 25% of the amount exceeding AZN 2,500.

Corporate Income Tax:

- A flat rate of 20% for most businesses.

- Simplified tax regimes with lower rates (2% or 8%) are available for small businesses and businesses in certain sectors.

- Additional taxes may be levied on specific industries, such as mining and natural resources.

Value Added Tax (VAT):

- Standard rate of 18% on most goods and services.

- Reduced rates of 0% and 7% apply to certain essential goods and services.

  https://www.taxes.gov.az/

Free market agreements:

Azerbaijan's free trade agreements (FTAs):

Bilateral FTAs:

- Turkey: Signed in 1992, this FTA eliminates tariffs on most goods traded between the two countries. It has been a major driver of economic growth for both nations.

LLC Comparator

CIS member states:

Azerbaijan has FTAs with several CIS member states, including Russia, Ukraine, Georgia, Kazakhstan, Kyrgyzstan, Tajikistan, Uzbekistan, Moldova, and Belarus. These agreements generally eliminate tariffs on goods originating from the respective countries.

- Iran: An FTA with Iran was signed in 2016 but has not yet been ratified by both countries.

Regional FTAs:

- Turkmenistan-Azerbaijan-Iran: This trilateral FTA is currently under negotiation.

Other trade agreements:

- Azerbaijan has observer status at the World Trade Organization (WTO) and is in the process of negotiating accession.
- Azerbaijan is also a member of several regional trade agreements, such as the Black Sea Economic Cooperation Organization (BSEC) and the Shanghai Cooperation Organization (SCO).

Salary levels.

$ 494

Reputation and Corruption levels.

According to Transparency International's 2017 Corruption Perceptions Index (CPI), Azerbaijan achieved its best position since 2000 with a score of 31.

Citizenship options by company registration.

No direct citizenship is given by them >>>>>>>>>

https://www.migration.gov.az/ru

Foreign ownership?

Yes

Physical address needed?

Yes

Local hiring needed?

No

What documents do I need to provide?

Application form: Provided by the Ministry of Taxes, the registration authority for legal entities.

Incorporation documents: Including the charter of the company, the resolution of shareholders on the establishment of the LLC, and the appointment of a legal representative.

LLC Comparator

Articles of association: These describe the company's structure, shareholders, and business activities, and must be prepared in Azerbaijani.

Incorporation decision of shareholders: This is one of the company incorporations documents.

Proof of payment of registration fees: This includes the receipt evidencing payment of the state registration fee and charter capital.

Copies of the owner's documents: These should be prepared, and the shareholder's signature should be notarized.

Information about the firm's business address: This should be provided, and a bank account should be opened.

Web Reference for web sourcing.

- State Registration Service of the Republic of Azerbaijan:

  https://e-gov.az/

- Ministry of Taxes of the Republic of Azerbaijan:

  https://www.taxes.gov.az

Chamber of Commerce and Industry of the Azerbaijan Republic:

LLC Comparator

https://www.chamber.az/static/azerbaijan_chamber_commerce_industry

LLC Comparator

Country: Pakistan

LLC Registration price:

The minimum amount of authorized capital for registering a company in Pakistan is PKR 100,000. This is around US\$823.

Tax levels:

Income tax slabs in Pakistan are based on an individual's annual taxable income. The slabs are determined by the amount of income earned during the year. The government of Pakistan has finalized tax slabs for salaried individuals for the fiscal year 2022-23 and has set a minimum income tax rate of 2.5% for those earning up to Rs. 100,000 per month and a maximum of 35% for individuals earning a monthly salary over Rs.1 million.

Free market agreements:

Pakistan's Free Trade Agreements and Partnerships:

Full Free Trade Agreements:

- China-Pakistan Free Trade Agreement (CPFTA)
- Pakistan-Sri Lanka Free Trade Agreement (SLFTA)

- Malaysia-Pakistan Free Trade Agreement (MPFTA)

Preferential Trade Agreements (PTAs)

- South Asian Free Trade Area (SAFTA)
- Indonesia-Pakistan Preferential Trade Agreement (IPTA)
- Iran-Pakistan Preferential Trade Agreement (IPTA)
- Turkey-Pakistan Preferential Trade Agreement (TPTA)
- Mauritius-Pakistan Preferential Trade Agreement (MPTA)

https://www.commerce.gov.pk/about-us/trade-agreements/

Salary levels.

24,028 PKR (around USD 180)

Reputation and Corruption levels.

In 2021, Pakistan was ranked 140th out of 179 countries in the CPI

Citizenship options by company registration.

No, Direct citizenship is offer after registration >>>>>>
https://www.interior.gov.pk/

Foreign ownership?

Yes

Physical address needed?

Yes

LLC Comparator

Local hiring needed?

No

Time needed for registration.

4–6 weeks (about 1 and a half months).

What documents do I need to provide?

1. Filled form I.

2. Bank challan of prescribed Registration fee.

3. CNIC copies of all partners and CNIC of all witnesses.

4. Copy of all the above documents duly notarized by a notary public.

5. Rent Agreement or title document of the premises.

6. Last utility paid bill.

7. Memorandum of Association

8. Article of Association.

Web Reference for web sourcing.

- SECP Company Registration Guide:

    https://www.secp.gov.pk/company-formation/registration-of-company/

- How to Register a Company in Pakistan:

LLC Comparator

https://www.secp.gov.pk/company-formation/registration-of-company/

- List of Prohibited Zones for Company Registration: https://www.secp.gov.pk/prohibited-words/

LLC Comparator

Country: Hong Kong

LLC Registration price:

The average business setup fee is around US ($10,105)

Tax levels:

Individuals are taxed at progressive rates on their net chargeable income (i.e. assessable income after deductions and allowances) starting at 2% and is capped at 17%; or 15% of net income (i.e. income after deductions only), whichever is lower.

Hong Kong is considered a leading tax haven due to its laws that limit taxation on the island's wealthy foreign residents and corporations.

In fact, in 2020, accounting firm PwC and the World Bank ranked Hong Kong as the country with the friendliest tax system.

Free market agreements:

Hong Kong boasts a robust network of free trade agreements (FTAs) that have been instrumental in its economic success.

1. Mainland China Closer Economic Partnership Arrangement (CEPA):

2. Agreement on Economic and Technical Cooperation (AETC) with ASEAN:

3. Free Trade Agreements with other countries:

- Hong Kong has also signed FTAs with several other countries, including <u>Australia, Chile, New Zealand, and the European Free Trade Association (EFTA).</u>

<u>https://www.trade.gov/knowledge-product/hong-kong-macau-trade-agreements</u>

<u>Salary levels.</u>

$3,219

Reputation and Corruption levels.

According to the 2022 Corruption Perceptions Index (CPI), Hong Kong is the 12th least corrupt country out of 180 countries and territories.

<u>Citizenship options by company registration.</u>

No, direct citizenship is given by Hong Kong

>>>>>>>><u>https://www.immd.gov.hk/</u>

Foreign ownership?

Yes

Physical address needed?

Yes

Local hiring needed?

No

Time needed for registration.

5–10 working days.

What documents do I need to provide?

1. Articles of Association

2. Completed incorporation form

3. Notice for the Business

4. Registration Office

5. Share capital details and information about shareholders

6. English translations, where applicable

Web Reference for web sourcing.

Hong Kong Companies Registry:

https://www.cr.gov.hk/en/home/index.htm

LLC Comparator

InvestHK:

https://www.investhk.gov.hk/en/

Business Registration Certificate Online:

https://www.gov.hk/en/residents/

LLC Comparator

Country: Egypt

LLC Registration price:

The minimum capital required for an LLC is EGP 50,000 (approximately USD 3,100).

Tax levels:

Egypt's tax system is diverse and can vary depending on the type of taxpayer and their income source. Here's a breakdown of the key tax levels:

Individual Taxes:

- Progressive Income Tax: Rates range from 5% to 25% based on annual income.
- Social Security Contributions: Employees contribute 11% of their salary, and employers contribute an additional 14%.
- Capital Gains Tax: 15% of profits from selling property or other assets.
- Inheritance Tax: Applies to inheritances exceeding 2 million EGP, with rates ranging from 2% to 4%.

Corporate Taxes:

- Corporate Income Tax: Flat rate of 22.5% on net taxable profits.
- Withholding Taxes: 10% or 5% imposed on dividends paid to resident corporate shareholders.
- VAT (Value Added Tax): Standard rate is 14%, with a reduced rate of 5% for essential goods and machinery.

Other Taxes:

- Real Estate Tax: Varies depending on property type and location, typically ranging from 2% to 4% of the property value.
- Customs Duties: Applied to imported goods at varying rates depending on the type of goods.

https://taxsummaries.pwc.com/egypt

Free market agreements:

Egypt boasts a network of free trade agreements (FTAs) that provide preferential access to markets and boost its trading opportunities. Here's a breakdown of some key agreements:

Multilateral Agreements:

- General Agreement on Tariffs and Trade (GATT)

LLC Comparator

- General Agreement on Trade in Services (GATS):
- African Continental Free Trade Area (AfCFTA):

Regional Agreements:

- Euro-Mediterranean Partnership:
- Greater Arab Free Trade Area (GAFTA):
- Common Market for Eastern and Southern Africa (COMESA):
- Agadir Agreement: Creates an FTA among Egypt, Morocco, Tunisia, and Jordan, focusing on promoting intra-regional trade in industrial goods.

Bilateral Agreements:

- Egypt-Turkey Free Trade Agreement:
- Egypt-EFTA Free Trade Agreement: Provides duty-free access to the EFTA markets of Iceland, Norway, Switzerland, and Liechtenstein for most Egyptian industrial goods.
- Egypt-MERCOSUR Free Trade Agreement: Opens access to the South American trade bloc for Egyptian goods, particularly textiles and chemicals.

Salary levels.

$303
LLC Comparator

Reputation and Corruption levels.

According to Transparency International's 2022 Corruption Perceptions Index, Egypt scored 30 out of 100, ranking 130th out of 180 countries.

Citizenship options by company registration.

No, direct citizenship is given by country >>>>>>>>>>>
https://mof.gov.eg/en/

Foreign ownership?

Yes

Physical address needed?

Yes

Local hiring needed?

No

Time needed for registration.

3 – 4 weeks from the date of submitting documents

What documents do I need to provide?

1. Notarized POA from all partners.

2. Copies of valid ID or passports of founders.

3. Original certificate from the register of accountants and auditors.

LLC Comparator

4. Certificate certifying name approval by the commercial registry.

5. Name and Address proof of the company's legal consultant.

<u>Web Reference for web sourcing.</u>

Ministry of Trade and Industry (MTI):

http://www.mti.gov.eg/

Egyptian Unified Register Center (URC):
https://www.goeic.gov.eg

Invest in Egypt:

https://www.investinegypt.gov.eg/

  PwC Egypt:

https://www.pwc.com/m1/en/about-us/office-locations-middle-east/egypt.html

LLC Comparator